BRITAIN IN OLD PHOTOGRA…

# ROMNEY MARSH

## A SECOND SELECTION

EDWARD CARPENTER

SUTTON PUBLISHING LIMITED

Sutton Publishing Limited
Phoenix Mill · Far Thrupp · Stroud
Gloucestershire · GL5 2BU

First published 1996



**British Library Cataloguing in Publication Data**
A catalogue record for this book is available from the British Library.

ISBN 0-7509-1152-2

Typeset in 10/12 Perpetua.
Typesetting and origination by
Sutton Publishing Limited.
Printed in Great Britain by
Ebenezer Baylis, Worcester.

This book is dedicated to my two
grandsons, Jack William Price
and Zachary James Cole.

# CONTENTS

George Tart wearing the uniform of a Bird Watcher, whilst working for the Royal Society for the Protection of Birds on their reserve at Dungeness, *c*. 1930. In 1947 he wore another cap, that of Coxswain of the Dungeness Lifeboat, a position he held for eighteen years. He was awarded the RNLI Bronze Medal in 1956 for his part in the MV *Teeswood* rescue.

# INTRODUCTION

This sequel to my previous book *Romney Marsh in Old Photographs* covers a period of almost a hundred years up to and including 1965. This allows a combination of pictures dating back to the last century along with ones in which people and scenes will be recognizable and in the memory of many present-day readers.

Farming has always been of prime importance and a principal means of earning a living on the Marsh, so there are photographs showing not just the men ploughing, planting, reaping and seed-stomping in the days of horse power, but also the women working alongside in the fields, in addition to their tasks of running a home and raising the children. And because of the long association the area has with sheep farming, dating from a Saxon charter of 697 AD, and still continuing today, with grazing making up one-third of Romney Marsh, I have given shepherds and shearers their own chapter.

Later pictures, especially those taken after the Second World War, chronicle the rapid rate of mechanization. In the name of progress tractors superseded the farm horses, which had nearly all disappeared by the mid-fifties.

In contrast, and doubtfully in the service of progress, the Marsh's branch railway, opened in 1881 and here seen in action, fell victim to the Beeching axe, fully closing in 1967.

Early attempts by the Royal Flying Corps to emulate the birds appear side by side with views of the then modern Bristol Freighters which played a leading role in the meteoric rise of the new Lydd Airport, ferrying thousands of people and cars to the Continent.

There is no denying that probably the most notable change in Romney Marsh was brought about by the decision to build two nuclear power stations at Dungeness. The first, Dungeness 'A', planned and begun in 1958, was completed and generating by September 1965, and brought with it, both in construction and operation, much-needed jobs at a time when machines were elbowing workers off the land.

The photographs are not all about jobs and development. Before the age of the television and video recorder – and the radio, for that matter – people made their own entertainment and took part in sports instead of just watching them. And so there were pictorial records of both players and fun days.

Romney Marsh has a long history, colourful traditions, unspoilt villages and a countryside rich in fauna and flora. This book is a celebration of a century of Marsh life, in all its forms; a blend of social history and sheer nostalgia. Things are still changing, one hopes for the better. Perhaps this can serve as a bench-mark to monitor that progress.

A picturesque rural scene in early spring near Brookland in the late 1950s. The Romneys are shown grazing on what little grass there is, supplemented by food in the troughs. Already at this period many acres of pasture land had been ploughed, and the post-and-rail fencing was disappearing, to be replaced by netting; where arable land predominates fencing today no longer exists. The hawthorns, along with the willows and blackthorn, help to break up what would otherwise be a bleak scene indeed.

*SECTION ONE*

# TOWNS AND VILLAGES

The aerial views of our three main towns illustrate how much change has taken place in such a relatively short period. The smaller villages have perhaps not fared particularly well, having lost many shops and tradesmen, while population has increased. Even so, all the towns and villages still retain much of their charm and character, and it is always a pleasure to visit the Romney Marsh churches, which have a fame reaching far beyond their immediate area.

*This country village entrance to Newchurch, c. 1920, shows a narrow road built for a slower pace of traffic. The sign indicates the school which stood around the corner, but, as in many of our villages, the school has gone, along with such signs.*

A pastoral view of New Romney, *c.* 1951. This aerial photograph was taken before the post-war expansion of the borough. Using the tower of St Nicholas for bearings, one can see to the right the beginning of Churchlands Estate and the field by Church Road which has now become a very large housing estate. Looking to the left of the tower, most of the green spaces along the roads, except Neames Platt, have been built upon. There have been many changes, too many to list here, but look for the classrooms and canteen built for Southlands in Mill Road, the area of the school playing fields in Station Road where Southlands new school now is, and the low, white building of the Rural District Council in Rolfe Lane. Note the number of trees before the dreaded Dutch elm disease took hold, and appreciate this country scene from the past, with stooks of corn drying in the sun in the foreground.

An aerial photograph from the camera of Robert Finn, *c.* 1935, follows the A259 from New Romney to Dymchurch. High Knock bridge stands out, spanning the outfall sewer and leading to a large house and small farmyard. The tall building beside the bridge is a garage with chauffeur's quarters above. In the fields close to the village are the camp sites. In the first field a group of Scouts have formed a camp with an assortment of tents, the largest being the mess tent. This particular field later housed the Casino, but is now a large housing estate. Martello Tower No. 25 still stands, though no longer with its cannon on top. The wooden huts, which were brought from Shorncliffe Camp to be used for holiday letting, were known as Tower Gardens and were dismantled after the Second World War. The area around the tower is now a car park for visitors. Looking a bit further along one can see another Martello Tower in the centre of the village. Dymchurch these days is still attractive and has grown into a well-known resort.

An aerial view of Lydd taken in 1958. Before 1940 very little building had taken place for some years. The area shown top left was the first large development Lydd had seen, with new council houses built on land which was part of the ancient Rype and which has now been completely developed. Behind the school in Skinner Road can be seen a long, low row of wartime shelters awaiting demolition. Facing the school is the remainder of the once large Rype, a piece which has now been preserved as the village green. The gardens in Eastern Road, shown in the centre of the photograph, have now been inbuilt with houses. The high chancel of the church, destroyed by enemy action in 1940, shows the completed restoration. To the right of the church, in the High Street, can be seen the large building of Finn's Brewery, unfortunately now gone, while the meadows beyond have been lost to two large housing estates. This once rural village of Lydd has now taken on an urban appearance.

Park Street, Lydd, *c.* 1900. The most noticeable difference now is the change to the thatched cottage and farm building, for this was one of a number of small farms found then in the middle of country villages. Where the man is looking into the Platt is now the back entry to Lydd Fire Station. The Royal Oak, on the left, has altered little through the years.

Porch House, 1912. This was the oldest and largest house in Station Road, Lydd, dating back to the fifteenth century. After being damaged by bombs dropping nearby during the Second World War, it unfortunately had to be demolished.

A scene in Lydd High Street in the 1920s. The infamous Beehive Inn is on the left with the Hughes's butcher's shop next door. The Beehive has long been closed but the butcher's shop is still trading under different management. The owners of the cars did not face today's parking problems.

This large porched house, pictured in 1964 just before it was demolished to make way for Vyes's enlarged store to replace the one shown on its right, was the house of the manager, Mr Piper. The old grocery shop was sold. Next to it was the Music Shop, and further along was, and still is, Lloyds Bank.

A pleasant view of Station Road, Lydd, the entrance to the town from New Romney, 1961. Most of the trees have been lost through Dutch elm disease. Today houses line both sides of the road, turning a rural picture into an urban one.

The Parade, Greatstone, *c.* 1938. This road was established in 1935 and immediately house-building began in earnest on both sides at Greatstone. Today there is hardly an empty plot to be seen along this busy road.

A view taken from New Romney Church tower, *c.* 1885, looking down Church Lane. Three schoolchildren can be clearly seen in the school playground, and others not quite so clearly in the playing fields. The two white blurs are girls dancing, moving too quickly for the cameras of the time. On the left-hand side of the lane, where the thatched ricks are, was the farmyard where some of the film *Green Grow the Rushes* was shot (see page 122). Now it is a housing estate.

The Avenue, Littlestone, *c.* 1915, looking towards the sea. The owner of this prestigious car happily poses for the photographer. This part of the Marsh attracted many wealthy and influential people at this time.

A busy time at the Warren Inn, New Romney, *c.* 1905, with a shooting party with guns and dogs probably having arrived in the wagonette. The draper, T. Mayhams, was a familiar sight as he sold his wares all round Romney Marsh.

New Romney High Street, *c.* 1909. At the time of writing this caption, the weather is the same, but replace the horse and cart with at least twelve cars, and Soul House with a large garage.

The Coast Stores and Post Office, *c.* 1936. This shop once stood on the Dungeness to Lydd-on-Sea road near the RHDR crossing and is now a private house. On the left of the picture can be seen the remains of the old Napoleonic fort.

The Tea Rooms, Dungeness, seen here in about 1937, stood near the lighthouse and provided a welcome place to sit and rest over a nice cup of tea after strenuous walking across the shingle.

A view from Martello Tower No. 23, looking towards Dymchurch from Hythe, 1912. The area is still a green field but much better drained than the picture shows. In the distance can be seen the Oval, the place where the first German spies were caught on 3 September 1940 by soldiers of the Somerset Light Infantry.

A view leading to Mill and Eastbridge Roads at Dymchurch, *c.* 1912, the road to the left leading to where the Dymchurch smock mill had stood, hence the name. The other road led to the Manor of Eastbridge, which once had two churches, only the ruins of one being still in existence.

Dymchurch Bus Station, *c.* 1925. This was a very busy area in the summer, not only for boarding and alighting from a bus but with a large restaurant and cinema catering for the many people visiting the town and sands.

R. Uden's butcher's shop, Dymchurch, *c.* 1912. It was usual at Christmas to see meat hanging on the outside of the shop. Holly and flowers can be seen decorating the shop and its display of meat and sausages. The cold weather would deter the flies, but the local dogs could have been a problem. Mr and Mrs Uden and the errand boy gladly pose for the occasion.

Appledore Street, *c.* 1912. A picturesque view of Appledore, little changed today. In these early years photographs for postcards were usually posed, but Mr Avery of Appledore who took this picture just happened to see and record the boy falling from his bike. The postman obviously ignored any 'rule of the road', but of course there would be very little traffic.

Appledore Street, looking towards Appledore High Heath, 1912. The charm of this village has changed little, although there is more traffic today. Looking further down the street on the left, there is certainly a thing of the past, a tinker's caravan, with pots and pans and baskets for sale – once a common sight.

The entrance to Appledore from Stone, 1912. Ahead are Well House, Vine House and Church House, and the tower of St Peter and St Paul can be seen. On the left of the picture is the entrance to the village smithy. The chestnut tree, poetically connected to the village blacksmith, casts a shadow on hot sunny days, allowing him to keep a little cooler while working.

The Revd James Wilkinson MA in 1904, leaving the church of St Clement, Old Romney, after a service. The entrance to this charming church is through a porch which was built in the fourteenth century. The church itself is, of course, much older. In times gone by, people could be placed in or near the porch for burial. It was said 'to be buried in or near the porch ensured being near the path most frequented by the living, thus being kept more easily in mind'.

A view of the entrance to Brookland, 1912, a narrow lane, almost a cart track, running past the cottage known as Filberts. Because Brookland now has a bypass this lane is now almost as pictured.

Flooding at King Street, Brookland, *c.* 1930. Taking into account the fact that many areas are still below sea-level, this scene was not unusual before Romney Marsh was as well drained as it is today. In Brookland, King Street, as well as the 'Flots' near the Woolpack Inn, was prone to flooding in wet years.

The parish church of Brenzett photographed by George Wood of Hastings, *c.* 1904. This church is dedicated to St Eanswith, the grand-daughter of Ethelbert, the first Christian king of Kent. This picture was taken just after restoration work when most of the chancel was rebuilt. The young boy posing for Mr Wood is dressed typically as a country boy of the time, with long trousers, boots and gaiters. Viewing the church from this angle today there has been little change except that a dormer window was inserted in the roof of the nearside aisle in 1925.

The church of St Mary, East Guldeford, *c.* 1887. The house in the foreground is the Old Vicarage, barely recognizable today, having a large studio built beside it. East Guldeford Level is very reminiscent of how Romney Marsh looked at the turn of the century, with pasture-land and grazing sheep.

*SECTION TWO*

# FARMING

The old farming photographs in this section really speak for themselves, showing as they do the total reliance on manpower and horses, and how men, women and children were all expected to play their part, and most certainly did, especially with 'seed-stomping'. The tractor gradually began to replace the horse but the real turning point was the Second World War, when tractors arrived in numbers from America to help the war effort. Today there are no working horses on Romney Marsh, but there is some fine farm machinery performing the hard tasks which, in these photographs, employed far more people.

*Haying at the Wicks in July 1935. This area is on War Department land just inside the East Sussex boundary. The meads, as these areas were known, were tendered for by local farmers for the hay. Bill Gillett is on the load, Horace Gasson is beside the horse.*

Haying in the centre of Dymchurch, *c.* 1905. As seen in the aerial photographs, there were meadows and farmsteads right in the middle of the villages. This farmer is haying where Dymchurch School was later built, now demolished to make way for houses.

Ploughing with a balance plough in 1914 at Snargate, with three horses in line. Perhaps the use of a third horse was because of heavy-going while ploughing in turnip stubble, but maybe the middle horse was being broken in.

Reaper with two horses in 1912 at Snargate, harvesting a good crop of wheat. The machine had a narrow cutting blade, as a larger one would require three horses. Two men were needed on the binder; the man in white was probably the farmer.

Jack Apps and Jackie Buckley with Bill and Punch, 1949. Children growing up in the countryside in these years had the chance of making friends with cart-horses and the wagoners. Jack Apps was a particular favourite, always patient and willing to answer questions. Many times we would rush down to the fields to ride Bill and Punch back to the stable, to go into the hayloft, cut the chaff, and drop it into the manger. Jack was always generous with the locust beans, chewy but nice.

Cutting wurzel seed, 1955. Turnip seed was also cut in the same fashion, using seed-hooks. Bearing in mind that the seed-hooks were kept very sharp, this is obviously a posed picture, since the women, Joyce Hellier, Joan Fielder, Jean Huggett and Joyce Velvet, are far too close together.

The turnip seed has been cut and here is being loaded into sledges with the boys 'stomping it down' – hence the term 'seed-stomping'. After this it was carried to the sailcloth.

Threshing the turnip seed, *c.* 1925. The seed was placed on a large sailcloth and the horse and roller cracked open the pods, expelling the seed. A sack 'nappy' would be put over the rear of the horse to prevent any droppings from falling on the seed.

The sift horse, *c.* 1930. The newly threshed stalks were quickly moved to one side to allow the seed to be swept into one corner of the sailcloth, the sift horse being placed ready for the seed to have its first cleaning. Using a large shovel called a scubbit, the seed was put through the sieve several times. Once thoroughly clean, it was bagged up into two-hundredweight bags.

Horace Link with his Fowler ploughing engine, *c.* 1950. This, bought new in 1916, together with other steam engines owned by Link Bros of Rooklands Farm, Newchurch, was used for contract work all over Romney Marsh.

Ploughing at Maurice Ashworth's Farm, Scotney, 1946. Maurice Addy is driving a Fordson E27N tractor which is fitted with the DG4 half-track made by Roadless Tractors of Houndslow, Scotland.

Vic Cripps with his D4 caterpillar tractor and five-furrow plough competing in a ploughing match at Burmarsh in 1955.

Cutting hay at Scotney, near Lydd, *c.* 1948. Frank Armstrong is driving a Fordson belonging to Gerald Finn. This tractor, one of many sent over from America to help with the war effort, was a rather troublesome machine as it had been submerged in sea water when the ship bringing it over was sunk.

Frank Armstrong baling hay at Scotney for Gerald Finn, *c.* 1950. Two men were necessary to operate the Fordson tractor drawing the baler, which produced heavy bales tied with wire.

Planting potatoes in 1955 for Gordon Paine at Snave, using a three-row potato planter drawn by a Caterpillar D2, are Joan Fielder, Tony Mortley, Doris Dorman and driver Ken Ovenden.

Ron Sinden driving a Massey Ferguson in 1960, taking part in a ploughing match at Burmarsh. Points were awarded for Opening, Uniformity and Straightness, Packing and Covering Material, All Ground Ploughed, Closing Up and Finishing.

Prizewinners at a Ploughing Match held at Burmarsh in 1960. The Romney Marsh Ploughing and Cultivation Society held a match annually on various farms throughout the Marsh, all popular with competitors and spectators alike. *Standing, left to right*: Harold Jenkins, Len Newton, Jean Sinden (collecting on behalf of husband Ron), Joe Peterson (Champion of the Day), J. Piper. *Front*: Eli Frith and R.J. Morris.

Potato riddling, *c.* 1954, for Gordon Paine at Brenzett, a cold farm chore done during the winter months when the storage clamps in the field were opened and the potatoes sorted by means of the riddle, turned all day by hand. *Left to right*: Joe Wheeler, Joyce Cripps, Peter Spencer, Dave Ovenden, Bert Huggett.

Tea break, *c.* 1950. This group of women is having a break from asparagus cutting on Claude Paine's farm at Scots Marsh. Growing asparagus was first attempted on Romney Marsh in 1936 by a London company, Asparagus Estates Ltd, who negotiated with local farmers to plough their pastures and plant this luxury crop. It is still grown in the Brookland/Brenzett area today by a local farmer. *Left to right*: Mrs Mackett with son Tony, Mary Fielder, Mrs Clark, Mrs Elliott, Mrs Trigger, Flo Huggett. *In front*: Rose Baker.

SECTION THREE

# SHEPHERDS AND SHEARERS

The value of sheep on Romney Marsh is mentioned in the Domesday Book, and this area gave rise to a breed of sheep known throughout the farming world as Romneys. The photographs serve to remind us of the part played by the men and women who tended these sheep. By 1910 most shearers were using power-driven shearing units fitted with as many as six shearing heads. The shepherds, or lookers as they are known here, were joined by farm labourers for the shearing season. Women helped at lambing time and also acted as lock boy when shearing began. But two women, Maudie Lukehurst and Elsie Humphreys, actually became shearers, working alongside the men. Shearing competitions were held annually, with fierce rivalry, and one Marsh shearer, Les Ramsden, became British Shearing Champion in 1963 by shearing 390 sheep in a day.

*This photograph is a posed one taken in 1904 by Wood of Hastings, who assembled the shepherd, the sheep and a sheep-dog (left of the church porch), to bring together the five things which epitomize Romney Marsh: sheep, dyke, footbridge, looker and Fairfield church, one of the many small churches so typical of the area.*

Unloading sheep for washing at Westbroke in the 1920s. It was usual to wash sheep before shearing in order to remove some of the grease from the wool, a practice generally carried out ten days in advance. In the picture are Leslie Finn, Bert Bourne the looker, and Arthur Finn the owner.

The Huggett family shearing, *c.* 1920, with a portable engine, driving six units, made by Galls of Rye. Also powered by the engine is the grinder for sharpening the head, seen on the right-hand side, upright. The men, Tim, Alf, Bert, Mick and Johnny Huggett, would wind the fleeces as they went.

Marsh shearers pose for a photograph, *c.* 1920. Close inspection of the shearing machines shows that they are the old hand-turning ones converted to engine power. The petrol cans in the foreground have been painted white to show that they are used for water.

A Cooper Stewart shearing unit on a converted horse-drawn vehicle in 1958. Albert Reeves, Albert Flisher and Nelson Batchelor are shearing for G.T. Paine in Robin Hood Lane, Lydd. Dorothy Sisley is acting as lock boy.

Bill Sims with son Norman shearing at New Romney, *c.* 1963. The two shearing heads are driven by a Lister D engine with flexible cables, allowing the shearers more freedom to remove the fleece.

Ted Niedrich shearing for G.T. Paine at Snave in 1961. The lock boy waiting to mark the sheep as soon as Ted has finished is Trevor Ovenden. Once more a Lister D engine is driving a four-unit, but only two are being used, the other shearer being Bill Bennett.

An unusual looker for 1952. Maudie Lukehurst was a true looker, tackling every task performed by her male colleagues, putting in the inevitable long hours in the lambing field, the back-breaking task of shearing, and the management of the flock daily for the rest of the year in all weathers. The photograph shows shearing time at Carter Ground, Midley, with Maudie shearing in the traditional manner. On the right are the neatly rolled fleece of wool and the bag containing wool from lambs. Maudie's male colleagues are John Balcomb, Les Velvick and Johnnie Huggett.

Dorothy Sisley posing for the photographer in 1958. Although posed as shearing (which she could not do), she actually worked as lock boy, whose duties included marking the sheep once the fleece had been removed, having the Stockholm tar ready as treatment for any cuts, keeping the ground canvas clean, and any other jobs the shearers required.

A rural picture, *c.* 1958, when Jean Huggett became the lock boy at shearing time. Jean and the fine lamb happily pose for the cameraman in front of the windbreak, a necessity on the windswept marshes.

A New Zealand type of shearing shed in 1958. This was built by farmer Dick Merricks after a tour of New Zealand to study sheep farming methods.

Below the shearing shed, which was raised on stilts to keep the sheep dry. The animals were driven up a ramp into the shearing pens, and once shorn returned down the ramp to the field. Les Ramsden and Jack Pierce demonstrate the ramp and gate for the photographer.

The sets of shearing heads were driven by an engine outside the shed and three are being used here by Jack Pierce, Perce Poole and Les Ramsden. By the end of the season, 3,200 sheep had been shorn in this shed.

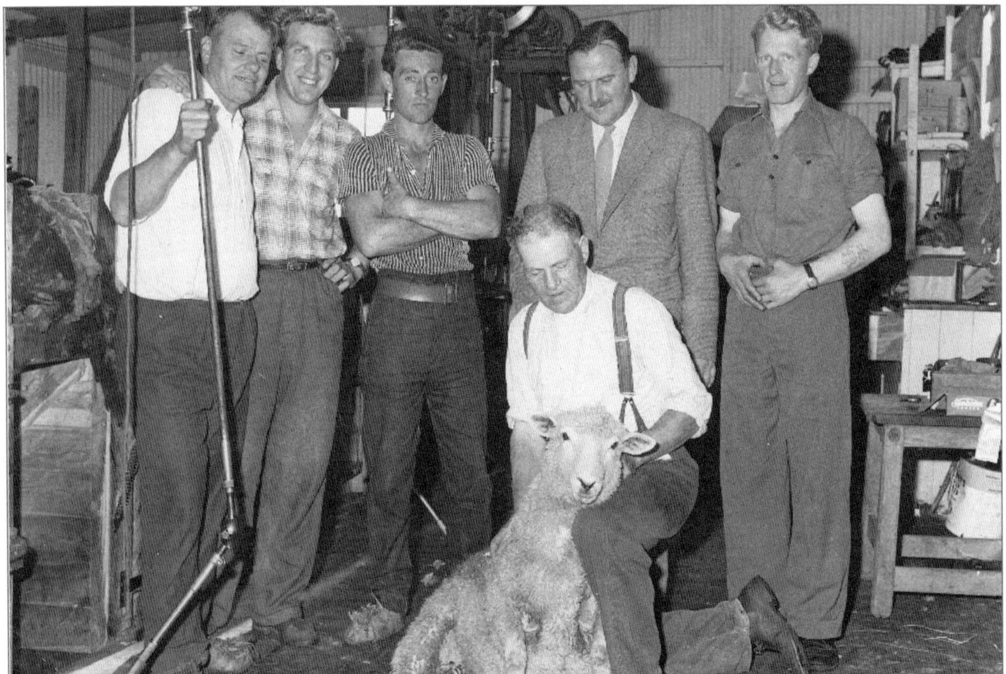

Representatives of Sunbeam Ltd meet the shearers in the new shed, *c.* 1958, to inspect the working of their machinery. *Left to right*: Phil Anderson (Sunbeam), Les Ramsden, Perce Poole, Bill Todd (Sunbeam), Archie Forest (Sunbeam) and Jack Pierce with the sheep.

Alf Huggett in 1929, judged to be Champion in his class for Shearing and Wool-winding when he sheared three sheep in 34 minutes at Caldecott Land, Lydd. He also won the cup for the best-shorn pen.

Jack Pierce receiving the cup as Champion Shearer in New Romney at the annual shearing competition, 1949.

Jack Jacobs, looker and foreman for Mr G.T. Paine at Brenzett, seen here with his four collies at shearing time, *c.* 1952.

A proud mother at Snargate in the 1960s. Twins are common and triplets are not unknown on sheep farms, and even the odd quads, but this ewe gave birth to six lambs. Mrs Joan Knight makes a fuss of them on Mr Dick Body's Vinal Farm.

*SECTION FOUR*

# LOCAL EMPLOYMENT

Although the majority of Romney Marsh people were at one time employed in farming and fishing, there were some who looked to other industries, and the pictures show some of the various jobs available. In addition to the brickworks at Lydd depicted here, there were other brickworks at New Romney and behind Dymchurch. Many people were employed at the military camps, some in the important task of keeping the sea at bay, and others in beach quarrying and at the brewery which later became the home of Lyddite Chicks. Today, however, many of the industries survive only in nostalgic photographs.

*Lydd Brickworks,* c. *1870. There were several brickyards on Romney Marsh. This photograph shows the workers in the yard on the Holmstone, an area now in the confines of Lydd Army Camp. It was still producing a small quantity of bricks until 1900. Holmstone Terrace in the High Street is built with its bricks.*

Staff of Finn's Brewery, Lydd, *c.* 1913, photographed outside Lloyds Bank, the entrance to the brewery being on the right. Edwin Finn began brewing beer in Lydd in 1859 and continued until 1921, when the business was sold to the Kent brewers Style & Winch.

The foreman sampling Finn's popular ginger beer, *c.* 1912, at the plant where this and mineral waters were made and bottled. The Finns sold the brewery to Style & Winch in 1921.

Hatchery staff at Lyddite Chicks, *c.* 1950. At this period this local firm was the third largest producer of poultry in Great Britain. *Back row, left to right:* Bob Godfrey (hatchery manager), Mike Allen, Tony Paine, Cecil Blacklocks (owner), Eric Boulden, Fred Winkfield, Ted Sharp. *Front row:* Margaret Tyrrell, Joan Stanley, Sheila Gillett, Betty Willicot, Shirley Spanner.

A typical scene at Lyddite Chicks, *c.* 1950. Bob Godfrey and Denis Wellstead are sorting the newly hatched chicks and packing them in boxes of 25 to be put on the train at Lydd station, destined for many parts of the country.

Littlestone Water Tower, *c.* 1900. This tower and works were built in 1890 by Mr H.T. Tubbs for his proposed housing development, the previous supply being from a pump in Littlestone Road. The Water Company at Dungeness now supplies the whole of the Marsh area.

The Water Tower, Dungeness, seen here in 1940, built in 1902 for the Littlestone and District Water Company. The black tower with its red top was a well-known landmark. It was altered in the sixties and now has a larger concrete top.

Water workers at Dungeness excavating beach for a new pumphouse at the water tower, *c.* 1905. Many local men were employed to lay the water pipes to Lydd and then on to New Romney.

The 'Wallers' pose for the camera, *c.* 1920, whilst carrying out repairs to the sea wall at Dymchurch. At this period rock was used to strengthen the wall, and groynes were built to break the waves and limit the damage to this most vulnerable sea defence.

Wallers, 1910. This was the name given to the gangs of men who built the sea walls along our coastline. These men are reinforcing the earth wall at The Brooks.

*SECTION FIVE*

# NUCLEAR POWER STATIONS

The idea of building a nuclear power station at Dungeness was first put forward in 1956. Test bore-holes were completed in 1957, and the public inquiry held from 16 to 18 December 1958. During the next year approval was given, and work commenced in August 1960, Dungeness 'A' Station being completed and starting generating by September 1965. This power station and the construction of Dungeness 'B' brought much-needed prosperity to the region (and indeed continues to do so today), for at the time agriculture was still undergoing more and more mechanization, with the consequence of fewer jobs for local people, while at the same time the peak of business at Ferryfield had been reached and its decline had begun. Today the stations are the largest employer in this part of Kent.

*Spindrift Cottage, 1958, once a fisherman's home, standing in isolation between Dungeness and Dengemarsh. It was demolished to make way for a much bigger structure – the nuclear power station.*

Construction of Dungeness 'A' began with drilling in April 1957, carried out by Wimpey Ltd, to test the suitability of the site.

In 1960 the real work of construction began when a large area was excavated and piles were driven down into the shingle for 34 ft. At this stage 500 men were employed and 2 miles of high fencing was erected.

The foundations for the turbine hall are laid. The large cranes were erected on site in preparation for the heavy equipment needed. Because water had seeped through the shingle, steel interlocking piles were driven down to a depth of 34 ft, encircling the area shown, forming a barrier against the encroaching water.

The Goliath crane, 1961. This 400-ton crane, with a lifting power up to 370 tons, was erected to extend the width of the reactor buildings in preparation for the very heavy loads from the pressure vessels and boiler units.

The Goliath crane, having served its purpose, was demolished by charges of explosive strategically placed on its iron girders in August 1965. This operation was carried out safely and all went according to plan. The RSJs taken from this crane now form the ramp for the Littlestone inshore lifeboat.

An aerial view of Dungeness Point, 1965, showing the completed 'A' Station and the construction of Dungeness 'B'. It also illustrates the shingle ridges which, over thousands of years, have built up this unique area.

*SECTION SIX*

# AVIATION AND FERRYFIELD

Romney Marsh played an early part in aviation, the Royal Flying Corps having airfields at Lydd (1914) and Jesson (now St Mary's Bay) (1917), with many other aviators visiting the Marsh, whether crash-landing when taking part in the Croydon to Paris race or building and testing aircraft as did Mr Alec Ogilvie at Camber. Lydd (Ferryfield) Airport, named 'The Car-Ferry Gateway to the Continent', commenced operation on 15 July 1954. Using Bristol Freighter aircraft, and later the Cavair, on an average day in 1965 400 cars and 1,300 passengers passed through the airport. Lydd Airport is still in existence, but is more known for its pop raves these days.

*An aeroplane of the Royal Flying Corps taking off from Dering Dome at Lydd in 1915. The cost of building one of these was £2,000 – somewhat different from the cost of an aircraft today.*

Between 1932 and 1938 air races were popular and this scene was not all that unusual, for seven planes crashed or made forced landings on Romney Marsh. This particular plane, flown by an RAF pilot, came to grief at Dengemarsh in 1938, the pilot escaping serious injury. Mrs Nell Prebble, with daughter Ellen, wearing backstays to negotiate the shingle, record the incident for the family album.

This Dove aircraft crash-landed at Dungeness on 17 January 1958. It came to rest between Leeside, home of W. Brignall, and Eastview, home of W. Tart. Belonging to Channel Airways, and on a routine flight between Rotterdam and Southend, it was diverted to Lydd because of fog, but didn't quite make it. The pilot was Captain H. Dennison of Essex. Fortunately nobody was injured. *Left to right*: Lydd Firemen Perce Olver and Joe Munds, Police Constable Clements and Police Sergeant Lowe.

The construction of the runway at Ferryfield Airport, Lydd, May 1954. It took less than six months to build and is 120 ft wide and 4,935 ft long.

This scene shows what a busy airport Ferryfield was in terms of aircraft movement. In fact it was one of the busiest airports in Europe. During 1965, 183,000 passengers and 74,000 vehicles passed through.

This aerial scene, *c.* 1955, shows the layout of Ferryfield, the road from Lydd crossing the Denge Sewer, with the petrol station at the loop. The main building and car-parks are in the distance and several Bristol Freighters are on the runway park.

Promoting both the airport and the Mini, this posed photograph illustrates that not only was it busy with ordinary passengers and their vehicles, but car manufacturers and dealers used Ferryfield to export their products to the Continent.

Queen Elizabeth the Queen Mother visits Ferryfield Airport on 1 July 1958, received by the Manager of Silver City Airways and welcomed by the Mayor of Lydd, Alderman G.T. Paine.

Film star Diana Dors happily poses with her large car while waiting for her flight to Le Touquet, France, *c.* 1957.

Dirk Bogarde arriving at Ferryfield with his Rolls-Royce in 1958. A great many celebrities used this method of crossing the Channel. A Bristol Freighter in the background is awaiting loading for yet another fast turn-around.

A somewhat misleading picture. Many German aircraft came down on Romney Marsh during the Second World War, but none landed as safely as these two, for they were taking part in one of the many airshows held at Ferryfield, this one in 1965.

*SECTION SEVEN*

# FIRE BRIGADES

It now seems most likely that New Romney formed a town fire brigade in 1846, purchasing an engine and dealing with fires in the town. But unfortunately no records exist telling how many years it was in service. We do know that by 1890 there was no fire service for Romney Marsh, so a brigade was established at Lydd to serve the whole of the Marsh. Dymchurch and Camber both formed brigades in 1936 to cover their immediate areas. With the outbreak of war Lydd and Dymchurch came under the Auxiliary Fire Service and a further group was formed at New Romney. Camber fire engine was taken to Iden, as Camber itself was evacuated and taken over by the military authorities. After the war, Lydd, Dymchurch and New Romney stations became part of Kent Fire Brigade as retained fire stations.

*Ancient and modern, 1952. The 1890 manual fire engine stands beside the new appliance of the Kent Fire Brigade outside Lydd Fire Station. The old manual engine was taken to the Fire Museum at Maidstone, but has now been returned and is in the Lydd Museum, in its old home.* Left to right: *Alderman G.T. Paine, Mayor of Lydd, a KFB official, and the Town Clerk, Leslie Winkfield.*

National Fire Service crew, 1945. Members of the Lydd Brigade at the victory celebrations on the Rype standing in front of the Dennis engine. *Left to right*: Rob Wellstead (captain), Steve Boulden, Frank Austin, Joe Munds, Wally Webb, Tom Else, Reg Browning, Ernie Frampton, Perce Olver.

Lydd Fire Brigade crew pictured in the old fire station, now the Lydd Museum, *c.* 1958. *Back row, left to right*: George Baker, Jack Haisell, Joe Munds, John Boulden, Bill Austen, Maurice Shepherd, Michael Allen. *Seated*: Wally Webb, Steve Boulden, two Kent Fire Brigade Officials, Rob Wellstead (sub-officer), Perce Olver, Dick Greenstreet.

New Romney Fire Brigade pose for a photograph in front of their engine, *c.* 1956. *Left to right*: Sid Morris, Les Paterson, Ron Miller, Harry Miller, Jack Polden, Ernie Adams, Sid Aldridge, Harry Davis, Ted Bolton, Bernie Messenger, Harry Clayson, Drummer Day.

The opening of New Romney Fire Station in 1956. The firemen present are Jack Bourne, Harry Clayson, Sid Morris, Bernie Messenger, Harry Miller, Les Patterson, Ron Miller, Drummer Day, Harry Davis, Jack Polden, Sid Aldridge, Ted Boulton and Ernie Adams. The officers are from the Kent Fire Brigade.

Dymchurch firemen in 1964 outside the old fire station in Orgarswick Avenue. Accompanied by two senior officers the chief Kent officer is presenting long-service medals to Sidney Checksfield (sub-officer), Brian Francis, Ernie Checksfield, Percy Divers, Percy Button, Sidney Jones, Percy King, 'Son' Mickleborough and George Warren. Les Stickells, a new recruit, stands at the rear.

Remains of the Lydd Camp gymnasium in 1958 after one of the largest fires that all three of the Marsh Brigades attended. Late in the evening of 3 August an arsonist set fire to this and other buildings, but this was the only one to be completely destroyed.

*SECTION EIGHT*

# ROYAL NATIONAL LIFEBOAT INSTITUTION

In the past, hundreds of vessels have been wrecked on our coastline and hundreds of lives have been lost or put in peril. The toll would have been much higher had it not been for the efforts of the brave men manning the lifeboats of the Royal National Lifeboat Institution. The scenes depicted here of Littlestone and Dungeness lifeboats and their crews and launchers mark the fact that the Marsh has long produced both men and women prepared to risk their own lives to save others – a tradition that continues to the present day.

*The Lady Launchers pose in front of the Dungeness lifeboat* RAOB, *1912.* Standing, left to right: *Lottie Tart, Mrs Deer, Madge Tart, Mrs Rebecca, Mrs Welfare, Anne Tart.* Seated: *Nellie Tart, Dorothy Tart, Amelia Tart.*

The Littlestone lifeboat *James Stevens No. 11* returns from a practice launch on 2 August 1909. This was the fourth lifeboat to serve this station and was a 35 ft self-righter, donated from the legacy of Mr James Stevens of Birmingham.

The launching of the Littlestone lifeboat in 1913 on a practice launch just after its arrival. During her sixteen years at Littlestone her records show only three service launches. In 1928 she was moved to Hythe and the station closed. In 1966 the RNLI placed an Inshore Rescue boat at Littlestone and this continues to perform an excellent service on our busy coastline.

The lifeboat *Charles Cooper Henderson* in 1952 with its crew and launchers ready for action in the Lifeboat House at Dungeness. *Back row, left to right*: Albert Haines, John Oiller, Ben Tart, Alexander (Son) Oiller, Fred Richardson, George Tart (coxswain), Archie Oiller, Joe Oiller. *Front row*: Jack Oiller, Den Oiller, Ellen Tart, Madge Tart, Sylvia Oiller, Pat Oiller, Edith Oiller, Doris Tart, Serena Fair, Charlie Richardson.

The Dungeness lifeboat *Mabel E. Holland* being launched by Mrs Francis after the naming ceremony on 14 September 1957. Built at a cost of £29,000, she could carry 100 people in good weather and 75 in rough conditions.

The crew of the *Mabel E. Holland* pictured in the lifeboat on the day of her naming – 14 September 1957. *Left to right*: John Oiller, Fred Richardson, Tom (Ben) Tart (second coxswain), Jimmy Tart, Bob Tart, Alexander (Son) Oiller, John Thomas, George Tart (coxswain), Archie Oiller, Albert Haines.

Presentation to Dungeness lifeboatmen of awards for services to the Motor Vessel *Teeswood,* March 1957. Coxswain George Tart received the RNLI Bronze Medal. *Left to right*: John Oiller, Archie Oiller, John Thomas, Albert Haines, -?-, Alderman and Mrs G.T. Paine, Mayor and Mayoress of Lydd, Fred Tart, George Tart, RNLI official, Alexander (Son) Oiller, Bob Tart, Fred Richardson, Will Thomas.

*SECTION NINE*

# LYDD LIFESAVING COMPANY

At one time all ten coastguard stations around the Romney Marsh coast had their lifesaving crews. These local men, all volunteers, assisted the coastguard in rescuing people from stricken vessels by means of rockets and breeches buoy. Lydd Lifesaving Company was founded in 1864 as part of the crew of Lydd coastguard station, which was at The Brooks, between Galloways and Jury's Gap. When the station was closed in 1891 the Company moved to Dungeness. It moved again in 1938 to Galloways. Then, because of the Second World War, it took over a new building in Galloways Road, Lydd, in 1942. In 1964 the Company was merged with the Lade Group to become the Coast Rescue Company. However, today there are no Rocket Companies on this part of the coast. George Newton, who served for thirty-seven years – sixteen years as Volunteer in Charge – was awarded the British Empire Medal in 1962. Longest-serving member was Steve Prebble, with fifty-four years.

*George Newton being presented in 1962 with the British Empire Medal by Ernest Marples, Minister of Transport, for his long and devoted services with the Lydd Lifesaving Company.*

Unloading the rocket apparatus from Turk's lorry, which was used to convey this lifesaving gear to whichever part of the coast it was required. *Left to right*: Dick Freathy, Frank Freathy, Ken Freathy, Bob Freathy, Steve Prebble, Albert Flisher, Norman Moon, Bert Pope, Bill Freathy, David Bourne, Tom Bourne, Charlie Williams, Bob Jones, George Newton.

A special truck with a large roller wheel used for conveying the apparatus across the shingle outside the Company store in Galloways Road. *Left to right*: Tom Bourne, Frank Tart, Steve Prebble, Frank Freathy.

Setting off with the roller truck which was towed by manpower across the shingle, in all weathers. *Back row, left to right*: Bill Freathy, Ken Freathy, David Southerden, -?-. *Front row*: Steve Prebble, Frank Tallis, George Newton, Len Prebble, Frank Tart.

Erecting the rescue hawser tripod in 1962. This would be done once a line had been fired by the rocket and had been secured to the stricken vessel. Helping to erect it are Ken Hewson, George Newton, George Baxter and Bert Pope.

Practice run in 1962. David Jones secures his son Glenn into the breeches buoy. In a real emergency Mr Jones had the task of wading into the sea to meet the buoy as it arrived.

Presentation to David Jones, watched by his colleagues at Galloways. *Left to right*: Bert Pope, Albert Fisher, George Baxter, Ken Hewson, Don Cloke, Len Prebble, Norman Moon, Ken Freathy and the full-time coastguard officers.

*SECTION TEN*

# DUNGENESS LIGHTHOUSES

The picture showing the first Dungeness lighthouse, which stood to the west of Dungeness Point near the Dengemarsh Outfall, is reproduced from a receipt dated 19 December 1630. The second lighthouse was built in 1635, on the site where the Grand Redoubt Coastguard cottages now are, remaining in service until 1792. Because of the constantly accumulating shingle a third lighthouse was then built for Thomas Coke of Norfolk, designed by Samuel Wyatt. All that remains of it today is the white base beside the fourth lighthouse, on which work began in 1904. The fifth and present lighthouse was a completely new design.

*The late Duke of Gloucester at the official opening of Dungeness's new lighthouse on 20 November 1961.*

The first lighthouse at Dungeness – a drawing reproduced from a receipt dated 1630. This lighthouse was shown on old maps as very near the Dengemarsh outfall.

This picture was taken from the original drawings for the coal-burning lighthouse at Dungeness built in 1635. It served Dungeness until replaced by the 1792 light.

The fourth Dungeness lighthouse in 1960, just before it ceased operation. Built in 1904, it is 143 ft high, with 174 steps to the gallery, and is now open to the public. The ground floor was used for church services and as a library for troops during the Second World War.

The positioning of the nuclear power station on Dungeness Point required the building of a fifth lighthouse, as the beams of the 1904 light would be obstructed. This new light, tall and slim, a completely new design in lighthouse building, stands 130 ft high and is constructed of pre-cast concrete rings which were made at Rye Harbour by Spun Concrete Ltd.

The completed 1961 Dungeness lighthouse is fully automatic, has a Xenon electric arc lamp of 300,000 candle-power and a range of 17 miles. A built-in foghorn, which is operated automatically by a fog detector, consists of sixty 100-watt loudspeakers.

*SECTION ELEVEN*

# LYDD ARMY CAMP

The first military camp was established at Boulderwall, near Dungeness, in 1879, but was used in the summer only. In June 1881 a permanent siege artillery camp was built, and through the years most regiments of the British and Commonwealth armies have been stationed at Lydd. The town also gave its name to the explosive Lyddite, tested here in 1888. Today, Lydd Camp is still actively used by the Ministry of Defence. Relations between the Army and the local population have always been excellent and remain so today.

*Open air service, June 1909. In the summer months, when several regiments of Territorials visited Lydd for training, there were far too many for the usual church parade in All Saints, so services were held on what was then part of the Rype. In the background can be seen Holmstone Terrace, York House and the Royal Oak. This part of the Rype is now the estate called The Green.*

The Artillery Camp, Lydd, 1912. The bell tents of the Territorials are in contrast to the brick barrack rooms for the Regulars. The officers' mess can be seen on the left and the clock tower and guardroom in the centre of the picture.

The Engine House, *c.* 1912, which housed the standard-gauge railway which ran from Lydd station to the camp and 5 miles within the camp. The Engine House, long redundant for locomotives, has been renovated and is used for other military purposes.

Local farmers delivering vegetables to the quartermaster of the Territorials at Lydd Camp, 1912. Potatoes, parsnips and cabbage were grown on contract to the Army. Large quantities of hay from all over Romney Marsh were provided for the military throughout the year.

A mock execution of a soldier in 1910 by troops of the Royal Garrison Artillery, presumably for some misdemeanour against his comrades. Photographer Arthur Shaw was there to record the event.

The arrival of the King's Own Rifles at Lydd, 1914. They are shown parading along the West End of the High Street, bound for the camp. The garage pictured is still trading, but the thatched cottage and shop, where the photographer Arthur Shaw produced his fine postcards, have long gone.

Corps drums of the 2nd Battalion Grenadier Guards, 1958, leading the Club Day procession through the High Street of Lydd. This Guards regiment was stationed at Lydd Camp at the time.

Church parade in 1928. The Band of the 3rd Battalion Royal Tank Corps is leading the troops to church, watched by many local people.

Armistice Sunday in 1954. Alderman G.T. Paine, Mayor of Lydd, takes the salute as the REME march past returning to camp from church parade. They were stationed in Lydd from 1947 to 1955.

A band concert in Elm Grove Field, 1913. One of the pleasures of being a garrison town in these years was that every regiment visiting Lydd had its own band, so there was no lack of music, with a band concert somewhere every week.

King George VI and Queen Elizabeth on a visit to the ranges, *c.* 1937. Being presented are General Sir John Dill, Brigadier Cummingham, Brigadier Thorne, General Alexander, Brigadier Carr, Brigadier Curtis.

*SECTION TWELVE*

# TRANSPORT

Transport has changed out of all recognition, both in the span of years covered by these photographs and during the succeeding years, with the landau giving way to the fast modern car, and open, solid-tyred omnibuses and charabancs to comfortable coaches. The roads they ran on, too, have improved from the bumpy, twisty lanes, dusty in summer and impassable in winter. The Romney Marsh rail link fell to the Beeching axe, but the Romney, Hythe and Dymchurch narrow-gauge line still gives pleasure to many people during the summer season.

*A very smart turnout for a local wedding in 1895, with Mr Alfred Gillett driving the landau belonging to his family on the West Rype – now covered in council houses. Holmstone Cottage and York House can be clearly seen.*

Daphne Unstead drives her milk cart past Brenzett School in 1931. The petrol pump was the forerunner of the large garage now at Brenzett on the A259. Daphne sold her milk from churns; although bottled milk was available from 1920 most dairies on the Marsh sold from the churn until the late 1940s.

An excursion from Brookland, *c.* 1913. This church outing to Margate would be the highlight of the year for people at this period, particularly for the children. All were specially dressed for the day. The straw boaters indicate fine weather with little wind, but 'hats off' was essential once the open vehicle started on its journey.

An early East Kent bus taking a group of schoolchildren to Camber Sands for the day, *c.* 1925. Camber at that date had only a few scattered houses. A nice Romany caravan appears at the back of the picture.

Mr Bill Allen with his motor-bus outside Lydd station, *c.* 1925. Joining his father's business after the First World War, he gradually replaced horses with motor vehicles. He had to pay the railway 25 shillings a year to operate from the station and was paid fourpence a hundredweight for delivering their goods.

George Palmer's lorry, photographed near his premises at New Romney, *c.* 1936. Mr Palmer traded as a butcher and farmer and was also an agricultural merchant. Although, as shown, he acted as agent for Vitamealo, he also milled and sold animal feed under his own name.

A busy scene at Lydd station in 1912, the down-train unloading passengers, including soldiers and their wives, whilst the goods train awaits clearance for the journey to Ashford.

A steam train leaving Brookland station bound for Ashford, *c.* 1930. As the picture shows, there is just a single track, the loop having been removed in 1921. This line from New Romney to Appledore was closed in 1967, but the line remains *in situ* as far as Dungeness for use by the power stations.

The Lydd Military Railway in 1911. The locomotive Nicholson brought 4.7 inch guns into the camp station for the Royal Garrison Artillery.

Dwarfed by the lighthouse, a train of the Romney, Hythe and Dymchurch Light Railway leaves Dungeness for New Romney, *c.* 1935. This miniature railway, the brainchild of Captain J.E.P. Howey, was opened in 1927.

Tragedy at Eastbridge Crossing in 1946. The Romney, Hythe and Dymchurch Light Railway has had an impressive safety record during its seventy years of public service, but in this case the locomotive Southern Maid was in collision with a lorry. Sadly, the driver of the lorry was killed.

*SECTION THIRTEEN*

# SCHOOLDAYS

These photographs are a reminder of our schooldays, whether recalled with pleasure or loathing. Most of us enjoy, particularly when getting older, looking at our own school pictures, even if only to remind ourselves that we were once young. In all the Romney Marsh towns and villages there is a reminder that a school existed – a building, a place name, or the school records. Today there are only six locations with schools, compared to fifteen at one time. Some had many classes based on age, while others had one class, with one teacher, covering all ages, but most had a photograph taken as a reminder of those days.

*Brenzett School staff and pupils, c. 1904.* Back row, left to right: *Frank Moore, Terry Upton, Herbert Moore, Ernie Mitchell, Bill Wratten, Percy King, Sidney King, Alfred Coy (teacher).* Third row: *Mrs Unsted (née Coy), Edith Moore, May Streeter, Mildred Ashdown, Daisy Upton, Bessie Nye, Winnie Nye, Rose Smith, Harriet Moore, -?-.* Second row: *Renee Ashdown, Nellie Wratten, Annie Wratten, Mabel Moore, Annie Mitchell, Mabel Mitchell, Lavinia Ashdown, Elsie Moore, Caroline Cottington.* Front row: *-?-, Fred Smith, Walter Moore, Fred Wratten, Claude Upton, Chas Moore, Baden Moore, Alfie King, -?-.*

Pupils and staff of Brenzett School, 1937. *Back row, left to right:* Mr Wilcox, Jean Huggett, Marian Everett, Robert Kent, Elsie Ovenden, Jeff Ramsden, Daphne Adams, Les Wilson, Jean Nichols, Ena Coleman, Don Dorman, Mrs Thomas. *Middle row*: June Elliott, Ivy Ovenden, Dorothy File, Harold Smith, Sid Fisher, ? Barton, Don Ovenden, Heather Wilcox, Stephen Rouse, Kathleen Adams, Cyril Adams. *Seated*: Keith Wilcox, Nellie Mackett, Stephen Adams, Bertha Humphrey, Jean Smith, Joyce Lancaster, -?-, Peggy Fuller, Bill Smith, Grace Heathfield.

Pupils of Dungeness School celebrating May Day with a May Queen and all her attendants, *c.* 1939. *May King and Queen*: Vic Rice and Jean Stewart. *Back row, left to right*: Daisy Tart, Don Richardson, Donna Oiller, John Oiller, Ron Oiller, Gertie Large, Elsie Allen, Joyce Read. *Front row*: Gwen Tart, Eric Oiller, Evelyn Allen, Sylvia ?.

Lydd School Football Team, 1925–6. *Back row, left to right*: ? Taylor, J. Williams, W. Grant, E. Frampton, C. Balcomb, F. Addy. *Seated*: R. Balcomb, ? Catt, -?-, ? Marshallsay, H. Whiting. *Front*: Maurice Shepherd.

Standard 4 at Lydd School, 1929. *Back row, left to right*: Mr Martin (headmaster), Billy Tye, Freddie Hodges, George Broad, Gordon Ditcher, Colin Leeds, Walter Webb, Leslie Ward. *Second row*: David Balcomb, Joyce Smith, Avis Martin, Dorothy Southerden, Jean Grant, Eva Tallis, Eileen Sanderson, Leslie Browning, Miss Keir. *Third row*: John Ansell, Doris Grimaldi, Brenda Bennett, Agnes Leadbetter, Maggie Whiter, -?-, Betty Apps, Fred Barnes. *Front row*: Alf Mannering, ? Reagan, Freddie Pope, Claude Burgess, Ernie Burgess, George Clifton.

Cookery class, Lydd school, 1937, a happy group of girls dressed for the lesson. *Back row, left to right*: Joan Apps, -?-, Nancy Pope, -?-, Betty Austin, Ruby Dennis, -?-, Dorothy Burgess, Maisie Vantom. *Middle row*: Lily Browning, Lucy Lambert, Evelyn Sharp, Mrs Cook, Mrs James, -?-, Elsie Mackett, Kathleen Genn. *Front row*: Edna Gillett, Joyce Mackett, Joyce Rainer, Margaret Gillett.

Pupils of Lydd School in 1953, all winners of a trophy and prizes at their annual Sports Day. *Back row, left to right*: -?-, Anthony Elliott, Pat Galloway, Janet Lowe, Heather Stribley, Michael Freathy. *Front row*: Angela Piper, Ann Heath, Roger Harrison, Michael Noakes.

New Romney Boys football team 1923–4. *Back row, left to right*: Tinker Southerden, Walter Gilham, Hugh Brown, Ernie Rabson, Jack Masey, Bill Reeves. *Front row*: Don Allen, Ted Hayles, Mick Petman, Herbie Summers, Roy Eldridge.

Pupils of Mrs Foreman's class, New Romney Junior School, 1959. *Back row, left to right*: Richard Wickman, Buster Gilham, -?-, Michael Knight, Neil Ramsden, David Suffrey, -?-, Graham Massey, Donald Crutchfield. *Second row*: Neil Reynolds, David Cripps, Malcolm Griffiths, -?-, Clive Parrish, Terry Gibson, Michael Rodgers, Richard Wimble, Timothy Rawle, -?-. *Third row*: -?-, Vivienne Ford, Janet Ellis, Elizabeth Arnold, Lesley Grant, ? May, Jackie Davis, Carol Fairhead, Janet Jenner, Yvonne Prior. *Front row*: -?-, -?-, Joan Longman, Ann Rootes, Marilyn Gill, Ian Cloke, June Longman, Janet George, Margaret Abbot, Wendy Fairhead, Alison Abbot.

East Guldeford School, 1907, with exceptionally smart pupils, a credit to parents and staff. Only a few can be named: *Back row, left to right:* no. 4 Fred Arter, no. 6 Frank Pilcher. *Seated:* no. 2 Charles Pilcher, no. 5 Ethel Hickman, No. 8 Rhoda Adams. *Kneeling:* no. 2 Ray Adams, no. 4 Cyril Pilcher.

The nature class at Brookland School, 1938. Study of nature and rural subjects was a priority in Marsh schools at this period, but sadly not so popular today. *Left to right*: Perce Pope, Pansy Blunt, Gwen Rye, Pat Frampton, Ivan Pierce, Perce Pools (feeding the goat), Don Smith, Don Clark, Stan Hickmott.

The entire school of St Mary in the Marsh posed for the camera, 1935. One young lady was asked to remove her hat, but she thought it so nice she refused. I'm sure you'll agree she was right! *Back row, left to right*: Ronald Noyes, Geoffrey Stratten. *Second row*: Grace Beer, Nina Burchell, Mary Burchell, Peggy McCullen, ? Rogers, Ray Arter, Bernard Noyes, Leslie Arter, Ray Burchell. *Front row*: Harry Beer, Dolly Sheaffe, Dorothy Sinden, Dolly Beer, Denis Arter, -?-, Freddy Young, ? Rogers.

Dymchurch School pupils, some in Scout and Guide unforms, *c.* 1918. *Back row, left to right*: Mr J. Brightman (headmaster), Kate Gosbee, W. Gostling, Renee Brightman, Cissy Uden, Evelyn Piddock, Tommy Young, George Warren. *Middle row*: Harry Newble, Nellie Groombridge, Ivy Butler, Gwen Piper, Florrie Gardner, Kitty Wraight, Dot Young, Lou Hoper, Reg Newble. *Front row*: -?-, Doris Rayner, Stan Wraight, Tony Philpott, Nellie Simpson, Chris Bartlett, Ronald Brewer, Lily Piper. *Seated*: Ernie Mitchell, Alf Bartlett.

The hockey team of Southlands School, New Romney, 1948. *Back row, left to right*: Yvonne Ashdown, Anne Boulden, Lilian Stickells, Nora Bennett, Eunice Drewitt, Margaret Miller, Peggy Couchman. *Front row*: Brenda Jones, Brenda Arter, Gladys Varrier, Mary Ovenden, Joyce Still, Mary Noakes.

Pupils of Southlands Secondary School, New Romney, *c.* 1951. *Back row, left to right*: Ray Gardner, Derek Hyde, Gerald Paine, Bob Anderson, Roy Beale, Peter Checksfield, Terry Piddock, Ian Tosh, Paul Rabson, Tony Akehurst, Billy Ellis. *Middle row*: Cyril Smith, Margaret Paine, June Croft, June Duncan, Jill Wraight, Rosemary Hamm, Gloria Wilkinson, Wendy Butchers, -?-, Audrey Adams, Eddie Baker. *Front row*: -?-, Betty Sargent, Frances Bull, Diana Sharp, Brenda Taylor, Mr Tullett, Brenda Fullick, Daphne Elliott, Shirley Nickolson, Merle Masey.

*SECTION FOURTEEN*

# SPORTING ACTIVITIES

If the men and women of Romney Marsh have always had to work hard for a living, they've played hard too. In the early part of this century goal running was as popular on the Marsh as is soccer country-wide now. Most towns and villages had a goal running team, and many also played the ancient game of bat and trap. Cycle speedway is another sport that more recently had its day and faded away, but cricket, football, golf and bowls still flourish.

*Lydd Goal Running Team, 1921, winners of the Bethersden and Dymchurch Cups.* Back row, left to right: *B. Pope (starter), J. Parks, W. Allen, G. Bourne, W. Godfrey, T. Marshall, G. Pope (umpire).* Second row: *C. Nickolson, J. Pope, H. Allen, L. Terry, H. Gasson, C. Makee, E. Paine.* Third row: *G. Burt (secretary), E. Woldridge, T. Prebble, W. Holdstock, J. Marshall (captain), W. Edwards, J. Sharp, B. Arter, F. Baker (chairman).* Front row: *E. Arter, A. Bushell, E. Edwards, T. Bushell.*

New Romney Goal Running Team, *c.* 1950. *Back row, left to right*: Bill Souten, Mr Snoad, Bob Bark, Jack Wall, Sid Ashdown, Harold Paine, Charlie Ralph, Jim Butchers, Joey Masters, ? Clifton, Harold Kirkland. *Second row*: Donald Ashdown, Doug Gillham, Bill Gillham senior, Bill Gillham junior, Joe Tye, Bert Tyrrell, Bert Paine. *Seated*: Chris Barnes, Peter Imbert.

The New Romney Ladies' Goal Running team, *c.* 1952, shown here with (in white) the Oare Team from near Faversham. *New Romney Ladies back row, left to right*: Marian Poldon, Leslie Paterson, Shirley Gillham, Valerie Wellsby, Marina Gillham, Joan O'Keefe, Linda Masters, Sheila Smart, Margaret Miller. *Front row*: Beryl Wellsby, Ann James, Mary McInerny, Ingrid Paine, Flo Gillham, Diana Sharp, Cynthia Bolton, Josie Tyrrell.

New Romney Football Club, 1955–6, winners of the Kent Junior Cup, Lydd Charity Cup, and Weald of Kent Charity Shield. *Back row, left to right*: W. King, M. Dray, B. Tyrell, F. White, B. Barlow, D. Aldridge, D. Apps. *Front row*: C. Pumphrey, W. Ellis, P. Webb (captain), K. Hunter, G. Gillham.

Lydd Football Team, 1948–9, winners of the Folkestone Junior League and the Weald of Kent. *Back row, left to right*: Harry Whiting (secretary), Wimp Balcomb, Eddie Gillett, Charlie Williams, Charlie Fagg, Squire Tordoff, Ted Bourne, Jack Bayley (chairman). *Front row*: Bill Wood-Brignall, Jim Noakes, Ted Frampton, Docker Williams, Frank Armstrong.

Lydd Football Team, 1951–2. Again a successful year, even with a few changes, winning three trophies – the Folkestone Junior League, the Weald of Kent and the Rye Charity Cup. *Back row, left to right*: Harry Whiting (secretary), Eddie Gillett, Jim Noakes, Bernard Ellis, George Bingle, Bill Flisher, Harvey Brattle, Rob Wellstead (chairman), Stan Murphy (linesman) *Front row*: Bill Wood-Brignall, Brian Lindsey, Taffy Huntley, Docker Williams, Frank Armstrong.

Dymchurch Football Club at the Sports Field, St Mary's Road, Dymchurch, 1927. *Back row, left to right*: Punch Piddock, Ray Smith, Les Haisell, Frank Ellis, Monty Upton. *Middle row*: Cecil Hopkins, Harry Waddell, Reg Newble, Jack Corns, Stan Wraight, Arthur Ford. *Front row*: Ern Checksfield, David Wraight, Ern Butler.

Brookland Football Club, *c.* 1954. *Back row, left to right*: John Mackett, Claude Ovenden, Don Clark, Tom Brooker, Dave Smith, Fred Lambert. *Front row*: Harry Pope, John Martin, Alec Beech, Dick Jones, Alan Elliott.

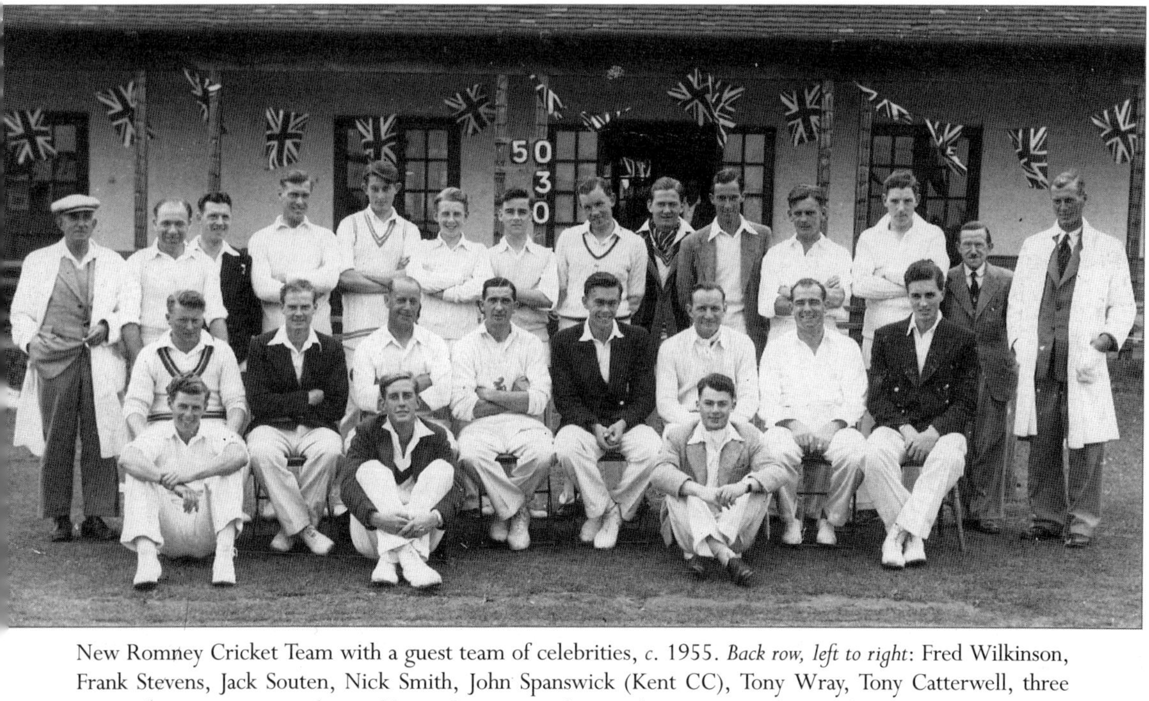


New Romney Cricket Team with a guest team of celebrities, *c.* 1955. *Back row, left to right*: Fred Wilkinson, Frank Stevens, Jack Souten, Nick Smith, John Spanswick (Kent CC), Tony Wray, Tony Catterwell, three guest players, Stan Ramsden, Eddie Holten, -?-, John Smith. *Seated*: Cecil Pumphrey, two guests, Eddie Crush (Kent CC), Simon Kimming (captain, guest team), Trevor Howard (the actor), -?-. *On grass*: Ray Murkin, Mike Cockran, -?-.

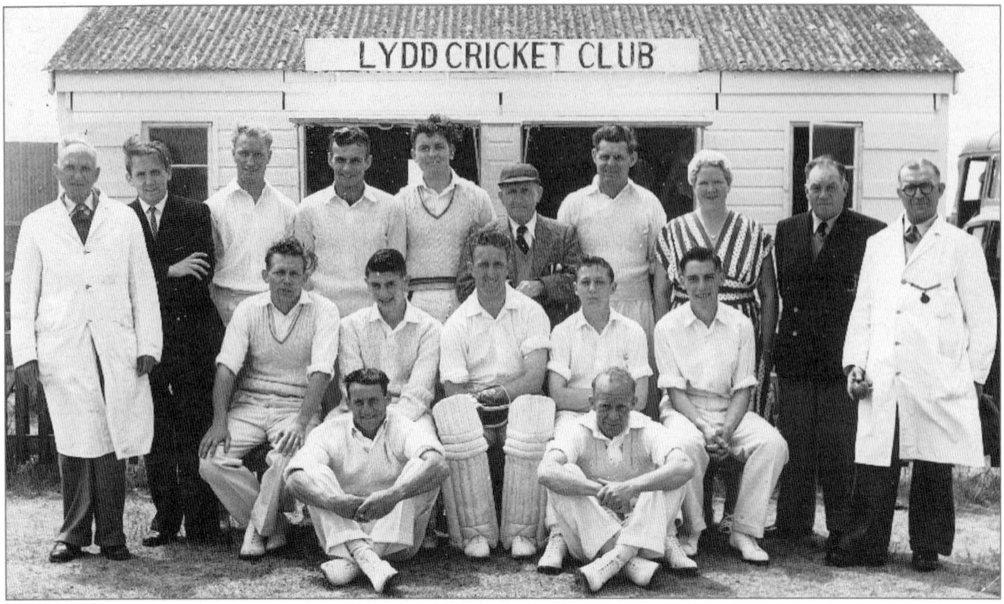


Lydd Cricket Club in the 1950s. *Back row, left to right*: W. Marchant (umpire), B. Clark, M. Lindsey, D. Walker, J. Adams, ? Phillips, J. Munds, Mrs I. Enser, A. Barnes, F. Adams (umpire). *Seated*: J. Clark, D. Bourne, D. Lindsey, P. Cobley, K. Spanner. *Front*: D. Burgess, F. Mannering.

Brenzett Cricket Team, July 1958, photographed outside their pavilion. *Back row, left to right*: Mrs Hurst (scorer), R. Christian, G. Fuller, K. Noon, B. Smith, G. Walton, D. Body, D. Clifton, P. Body. *Kneeling:* P. Ovenden, D. Moore, R. Clarke, R. Vincer.

Major Teichman Derville addresses the New Romney Bowls Club at their Club House and Green in Church Lane, *c.* 1937. The game of bowls has been recorded as being played for over a century in New Romney. The present Bowls Club is situated in Sussex Road.

Bat and Trap, 1949. This was an ancient Kentish game revived at Lydd by Bill Baines of the Dolphin Hotel. It has been described as the only game in which you can hold a pint of beer in one hand and the bat in the other. Shown is the Lydd British Legion Team: *Back row, left to right*: Dick Hickmott, Gordon Baker, ? Inder, Tug Wilson, -?-, Ted Frampton. *Seated*: Sammy Parker, Steve Prebble, Tom Kemp, Bert Markrett.

The Lydd Lions Cycle Speedway team, 1951. This team rode against a team from Glasgow. *Back row, left to right*: Brian Cooper, Bob Parkinson, Cyril Adams, Keith McTear, Tony Paine, Fred Cullen (team manager). *Front row*: Bill Webb, David Bourne (mascot), George Batchelor, Brian Lindsey.

Tee-off at Littlestone Golf Course, *c*. 1912, with boys and fishermen acting as caddies. The course was laid out in about 1888, the first competition being held later that year. The house now known as Netherstone, shown in the background, became the first club-house.

*SECTION FIFTEEN*

# WARTIME

By June 1940 the victorious German Army had swept west through Europe, the evacuation of Dunkirk had been completed, and the Germans now occupied the coast on the other side of the Channel. The Kent coast, and in particular Romney Marsh, was now Britain's front-line; invasion was thought imminent. The pictures depict just a fraction of the part played by the local population and the many members of the Armed Forces drafted into the area during those anxious years.

*Enemy action in Station Road, Lydd, 28 October 1940. These three houses were completely destroyed, but fortunately nobody was killed.*

Enemy Dornier shot down, 1 September 1940, in Tart's Field, Dungeness Road, Lydd, by Sammy Allard of 85 Squadron. The German pilot, Mathias Maossen, was wounded. Of his crew Wilhelm Illy was unhurt, Heinrich Wöhner wounded and Gels Speiss killed.

The crane from the local quarry helping to rescue Pilot Officer V. Ortman's Hurricane in 1940, when return fire from a Dornier caused a forced landing on the beach at Dungeness.

A section of the Lydd Home Guard taken at Ashford, 1942. *Back row*: Tom Stickells, -?-. *Standing, left to right*: John Linford, Ron Smithers, Jim Noakes, Alf Mannering, Ted Cooper, Bill Sims, Mick Broad, Ray Button, Nelson Batchelor. *Sitting*: Cyril Reeves, George Cullen, Albert Flisher, Charlie Elderkin, Jack Pope, Albert Flisher, Reg Browning, Reg Adams.

Members of the Royal Observer Corps at Brookland, *c.* 1940. They, with their colleagues at Dymchurch, Dungeness and Rye Harbour, played an important part in identifying aircraft during the Second World War. *Back row, left to right*: Harry Finn, Cecil Smith, Joe Sims, Jack Clark, Tim Santer, Bert Jempson, Len Newton. *Middle row*: Walter Smith, Sam Coleman, Mr Wilcocks, Jack Pierce. *Front row*: Ted Solly, Charlie Clark.

Schoolgirls Molly King, Jean Haisell and Margot Baker carrying their gas-masks on their way to school. Although Romney Marsh was very much in the front-line it was extraordinary how many children were not evacuated but continued to attend the local schools.

Civilian workers during gas drill at the Lydd Army Camp. The smiles on their faces show how much they are enjoying themselves!

*SECTION SIXTEEN*

# CIVIC AND LOCAL ORGANIZATIONS

The Lords, Bailiff, Jurats and Commonalty of Romney Marsh still meet annually at New Hall, Dymchurch – a tradition dating back to 1252. The Cinque Port status of New Romney and its Limb of Lydd may have lost its power but it retains its colour. The towns of Lydd and New Romney still have their mayors and the villages have parish councils, but the area of Romney Marsh itself now comes under Shepway District Council. Many other bodies are still going strong, with the St John Ambulance Brigade recruiting cadets at an early age for its Badgers, and Scouts and Guides flourishing in some places. The church organizations, such as bellringers and choirs of individual churches, remain. Sadly, though, there is no brass band on Romney Marsh, the nearest being at Hythe.

*Proclamation of the Accession of Queen Elizabeth II being read outside New Romney Town Hall on 8 February 1952.* Left to right: *-?-, Elam Ellis, Revd N.G. O'Connor, Charlie Cavey, A.E. Kirkland, Sid Morris, David Collins, Jack Wiles (Mayor), the Revd Mr Dolphin, -?-, Jocky Piper, Bill Smith, Ernie Prior, Tony Clinch, Joan Finn-Kelsey, Norman Grubb, Brian Ellis, Paul Abbott, -?-.*

The Proclamation of the Accession of Queen Elizabeth II being read at The Guild Hall, Lydd, on 8 February 1952. *Left to right*: Councillors Mrs M.F. Ford, W.C. Blacklocks, JP, Alderman T. Prior, JP, Police Constable Page, C.L. Winkfield (Town Clerk), Revd W. Britton, BA (Rector and Mayor's Chaplain), Alderman G.T. Paine, MBE, JP (Mayor), L.B. Wigley (Town Sergeant), Alderman H.J. Blacklocks, JP (Deputy Mayor), Alderman B. Prior, Councillor A. Wood.

St John Cadets with their emblem outside the old Fire Station at Lydd, now the Museum, *c.* 1930. *Left to right*: Bill Sims, Len Cooper, Bill Tye, Charlie Cracknell, Roy Winkfield.

The St John Ambulance Girl Cadets, Lydd, 1943. *Back row, left to right*: Mary Linford, Molly King, Christine Fowle, Eileen Beeching, Jean Haisell. *Second row*: Betty Sisley, Irene Smith, Eileen Stanley, Ivy Carpenter, Dorothy Holyer, Ann Turner, Jean Stickells. *Third row*: June Piper, Joan Weaver, Doreen Sims, Dorothy Sisley, Margaret Tyrrell, Jean Balchin. *Front row*: Doris Allen, Anne Adams, Audrey Carpenter.

Romney Marsh St John Ambulance Brigade, *c.* 1955. *Left to right*: Ernest Paine, Pam Thomson, Mary Parson, Mrs Cooper, Brenda Percival, Gillian Amos, Mary Parkinson, Basil Bourne, Ernest Ford, Tommy Stickells, Mr Cooper, Bill Bailey, Bill Sims, Norris Heritage.

Baron of the Cinque Ports Alderman G.T. Paine, wearing the chain of office of the Mayor of Lydd. Freemen of the Cinque Ports elected to attend a coronation are granted the honour of walking in the procession bearing the canopy held above the monarch's head, and are known by the honorary title of 'Baron'. Mr Paine had the distinction of attending the coronations of both George VI and Elizabeth II. Also shown are Alderman H. Smithers and H.J. Blacklocks and the Chaplain, Canon Collins.

Lords, Bailiff and Jurats of Romney Marsh, 1961. *Left to right*: Albert Link, Arthur Frith, Bill Smith, Anne Roper, Canon Bickerstaff, N. Owen, Major Krabbe, J.A. Duthout, Geoffrey Robinson, Major Teichman Derville, Spencer Buck, Frank Cook (Bailiff Sergeant), Dick Body, Gordon Paine, J.C. Allnatt, Henry Lordon, Herbert Blacklocks, J.W. Kennard, Bert Catt, Pelham Collick, Sidney Clements, Thomas Morse, Canon Hodge, George Boulden, Gordon Finn-Kelcey.

There are two separate corporations, the Lords, Bailiff and Jurats, who meet at New Hall, Dymchurch on the Thursday in Whitsun week, and the Bailiff and Jurats together with the Commonalty, who meet, also at New Hall, at Michaelmas. This was the only district in England with the right to elect its own magistrates.

The Lords, Bailiff and Jurats were responsible for the drainage and sea defence of Romney Marsh. This body dates back to 1252, and its charge was for the direction and control of works necessary to keep the sea out and the land drained, and to collect and set the scots or rates for the coming year. This ancient corporate body fulfilled its duties successfully for 678 years, only ceasing when the Catchment Boards were established under the Drainage Act of 1930.

The Bailiff, Jurats and the Commonalty were the body responsible for law and order on Romney Marsh, meeting annually to elect first the Jurats, then the Bailiff, and, from the Jurats, four Magistrates, reduced to three in later years. In the fifteenth century the Corporation was given the privilege of exercising full criminal jurisdiction throughout the Marsh, giving them the right to erect gallows, appoint their own constables, and maintain a gaol at New Hall. The Justices of the Peace Act, 1949, rescinded all these duties.

Both bodies meet annually in their respective months. Long may this ancient tradition continue.

The picture shows the interior of the ancient Court Room of the Bailiff, Jurats and Commonalty at New Hall, Dymchurch. *Back row, left to right*: -?-, Archie Wraight, Major Teichman Derville (Bailiff), Major Krabbe, F.T. Francis. *Front row*: Thomas Morse (Clerk), John Chapple, M.J.H. Girling (Town Clerk of Hythe), -?-.

Gang Show in Hythe, *c.* 1928. The combined Scout troops of this area put on this Gang Show in the theatre at Hythe. The photograph shows New Romney and Hythe Troops.

The Lydd British Legion Boys' Band, *c.* 1950. This 22-piece band was started by Mr Fred Pettitt, a well-known bandsman of the area. It performed at local festivities and concerts. *Back row, left to right*: M. Ralph, R. Catt, R. Dewitt, D. Hyde, E. Ramsden, G. Paine, P. Letford, P. Haisell, B. Mitchell, T. Carpenter, E. Baker, B. Carpenter, M. Wild. *Front row*: A. Duncan, K. Adams, M. Letford, P. Kemp, K. Wood, R. Ramsden, D. Bourne, B. Godfrey, J. Enser, Fred Pettitt.

Bellringers of All Saints' Church, Lydd, 1954. *Back row, left to right*: Bob Swift, Maisie Vantom, unknown, John Cooper, Mr Humphrey, -?-, Lew Terry. *Front row*: Christine Vidler, Olive Boulden, Anne Boulden, Margaret Terry, Phyllis Finch, Rosemary Marshall, Tim Finn.

The choir of All Saints' Church, Lydd, *c.* 1953. *Back row, left to right*: Mr Caspall, -?-, Mr Molden, Albert Terry, Mr Tullett, -?-, Arthur Balchin, Cecil Webb, Mr Sinclair, Bill Balchin, Mr Cooper. *Second row*: Leslie Winkfield, Mrs Vidler, Olive Prebble, Mrs Caspall, Mrs Mack, Phyllis Finch, Kath Mannering, Mrs Gillett, Thelma Balchin, -?-, May Tart. *Third row*: Michael Finn, David Ralph, Peter Kemp, Ralph Taylor, Bob Ward, Tim Finn, Peter Quinn, Mark Letford. *Front*: Peter Cobley, Tony Quinn, Christopher Adams, Terry Jones, David Bourne, Colin Smith.

*SECTION SEVENTEEN*

# FESTIVITIES AND ENTERTAINMENTS

During the summer period, organizations and societies were in the habit of holding some form of festivity. Brenzett and Lydd held Club Days – the latter still continuing – New Romney held its Revels and the smaller villages held their fêtes and carnivals. The Day of Syn at Dymchurch, which attracts large crowds, only began in the 1960s. Several feature films were made on Romney Marsh, mainly based on fictional stories, but still showing the characteristics of this unique area. The Marsh also has its natural attractions, golden sands round its shores, unusual flora and fauna. It can be seen that, before the days of television, the local population did not require anything very extravagant as amusement; community spirit was probably at its highest at the time of these scenes.

*Mr Busby of the British Legion crowning Carnival Queen Sylvia Huggett at Brookland British Legion fête in 1959.* Left to right: *Kay Smith, Mr Busby, Sylvia Huggett, Sylvia Tugwood, Frank Pilcher, Ken Smeed.*

Fancy dress competition in 1961 at the Brookland British Legion fête. *Left to right*: Laura Ovenden, Teresa Tilbury, Judy Pilcher and (lamb) Ben, John Tugwood, -?-, -?-.

Caught in the air. Jim Pilcher throws the horseshoe at the British Legion fête in Brookland, *c.* 1957, watched by his wife Molly and his children Alan and Judy, and also Stan Arter, holding his daughter Rosemary, all eager to see whether Jim's throw is successful.

Old Romney Sunday School children, *c.* 1937. These small concerts were always well attended, mostly by proud parents coming to see their children perform. *Back row, left to right*: Joan Balcomb, Arthur Paige, John Owen, John Mackett, John Balcomb, Basil Mackett. *Second row*: Kath Dines, Lily Mackett, Ena Huggett, Evelyn Owen, Toppy Mackett, Mary Paige, -?-. *Front row*: Margaret Paige, Beryl Batchelor, Dave Fielder, Bessie Huggett.

New Romney Ladies' Football Team taking part in Romney Revels with their male coaches, *c.* 1953. *Back row, left to right*: Bill Prior, Mary McInerny, Kay Smith, Sylvia French, Ann Fagg, Bob Barlow, Rosemary Rogers, Sheila Smart, Florrie Gillham, Joe Tye, Marge Smart, Billy Gillham. *Front row*: Linda Fisher, Beryl Welsby, Ann James, Margaret Savage, Betty Steel, Marianne Polden.

Romney Revels Queen 1953, Christine Walker, with her two attendants, is drawn through the crowd-lined streets of New Romney, accompanied by an Army Cadet band.

Nativity play at Brookland Church in 1951. *Standing, left to right*: Nellie Little, Vera Gardner, Joyce Webb, Iris Leeds-George, Lily Clark, Poppy Knipmeyer, Barbara Frampton, Rosie Brignall. *Kneeling*: Ernie Noakes, -?-, George Velvick, Ernie Brignall, Joan Hall, the two sons of the Revd P.W. Allen, Jim Pilcher, Dick Rome.

Cinque Ports Hotel tug-of-war team at Romney Revels in 1955. *Back row, left to right*: Jim Butchers, Walter Gillham, Dennis Gunnings, John Ford, Derek Frew, Ron Jones, Mr Chesty, Bill Gillham, Mr Fagg, Nibby Barnes, -?-. *Seated*: Les Malyon, Peter Webb, Mr Murkin, -?-, Maurice Belcher.

Romney Fairies receiving first prize, 1957, at Romney Revels from the Queen, Ann Paterson. *Left to right*: Barbara Tart, Jean Dray, Margaret Gillham. *The small girls*: Janet George and Sandra Bateman.

Selecting the Lydd Club Day Queen in 1958. Since the revival of Club Day in 1948, a queen has been selected annually – a difficult choice among the beauties of Lydd. *Standing, left to right*: Anne Reeny, Jacky Pritchard, Barbara Spanner, Pat Sacre, Ann Blechynden, Fay Clare. *Sitting*: Pauline East, Shirley Sims, Julie Harrison.

Lydd Club Day 1951 – the Ladies' Comic Football Team. *Standing, left to right*: Peg Pilcher, Ellen Ford, Molly King, Margot Baker, Joan Baker, Doris Mittell, Perce Brett (trainer), Connie Evans. *Kneeling*: Mrs Calloway, Marjorie Smith, Sheila Gillett, Joan Stanley, Clare Jell, Sally Waylett.

Doctor Syn coming ashore at Dymchurch in 1964 during the Day of Syn. It is probable that some of the ancestors of this villainous-looking crew actually took part in smuggling, which was widespread there in years gone by!

Day of Syn, 1964. This is the re-enactment of an episode from the *Doctor Syn* book by Russell Thorndike, a fictional tale of smuggling on Romney Marsh. The crowd, in carnival mood, is obviously enjoying every moment.

Local children at the St Mary's Bay fête in 1958. *Back row, left to right*: Anthony London, -?-, -?-, -?-, -?-, Peter Roberts, Cynthia Quick, -?-, Patricia Thompson. *In front*: John Roberts, Pauline Noakes, Judith Else, Valerie Ovenden, Sylvia Noakes.

Honor Blackman and Richard Burton were quite willing to be photographed by the inhabitants of New Romney during the filming of *Green Grow the Rushes*, *c*. 1950. As is known, they both went on to greater things.

Not quite as old as it looks! This is a scene from the film *Doctor Syn*, a smuggling tale by Russell Thorndike, which was filmed on Romney Marsh in about 1961, and here shows St Clement's Church, Old Romney.

Charles Southerden, a well-known Marsh looker, showing Chips Rafferty, the Australian actor, how to look as though he is shearing for the film *Loves of Joanna Godden,* 1946.

Beach huts at Camber had been erected by the mid-1930s, each with its fenced-in area. These could be hired just for the season or for one's holiday. There are no such facilities today, nor are cars allowed on the sands.

Summer days at Camber, *c.* 1925. As can be seen, the motor car gave the opportunity to visit places like Camber, which at this period had no public transport to speak of. The cars could be used as places to change and eat in, as well as for shelter from the sun, wind or even rain.

Children enjoying a Christmas party, *c.* 1950, laid on for them by Mr and Mrs Lambert at their premises at The Royal Oak, Brookland.

Comedian Tommy Handley declaring open the 1948 season on the Romney, Hythe and Dymchurch Light Railway.

# ACKNOWLEDGEMENTS

I would like to express my gratitude to Margaret Bird, for without her patience, advice, friendship and generosity this book would not have been written. I would also like to thank Harry Cawkell for reading and correcting the draft.

Sincere thanks to the following for information, advice and kind hospitality: Mr and Mrs M. Addy, Mr and Mrs F. Armstrong, Mr and Mrs J. Barnes, Dick Body, Mr and Mrs B. Bourne, Mr and Mrs D. Clark, Mr and Mrs D. Cole, Mrs D. Couchman, John Edwards, Robert Finn, Mr and Mrs B. Gillham, Mrs P. Gillham, the Staff of the Hastings Museum for the George Wood photographs, Bob Thomas of Haynes of Appledore, Mrs L. Hopkins, Mr A. Lackner, Tina and Diana of Lydd Library, Mr and Mrs D. Mattock, Mr and Mrs T. Miller, Nuclear Electric (Ann Bryant and Dr D.A. Spurr), Lt-Col. C.J. Parslow, Mr and Mrs J.C. Pilcher, Mr and Mrs J.F. Pilcher, Sylvia, Sam and Julie of Printing at New Romney, Mr and Mrs C. Pumphrey, Mrs S. Sharp, Mr and Mrs D. Sinden, Mr and Mrs T. Standen, Mrs E.L. Tart, and Mr G. Warren. Particularly, I wish to acknowledge the help and support I have received from my wife Chris and my immediate family.

My thanks and appreciation to the following for the loan of photographs (the numbers refer to pages, 'a' and 'b' to upper and lower respectively):

M. Addy, 28b, 89a; Y. Apperley, 94a; F. Armstrong, 29b, 30a, 97b, 98a, 123b; E. Atkinson, 54a; D. Balcomb, 89b; J. Barnes, 52a, 96a; D. Body, 29a, 42b; B. Bourne, 34a, 108b, 109b, 122b; I. Carpenter, 109a; D. Clark, 99a; D. Cole, 24a, 125b; J. Cole, 94b; P. Dark, 125a. G. Dawes 121b; J. Edwards, 7, 12a, 17a, 17b, 18a, 21b, 27a, 28a, 63, 77b; J. Ellis, 106a, 107, 112b; R. Finn, 9, 47a, 103, 104a, 104b; T. Finn, 114b; Friends of Lydd, 43, 44b, 72a, 81, 90a, 95; D. Fritchley, 124a, 124b; J. Gillham, 16a, 88b, 119b; B. Hutchins, 117b; D.G. Jones, 67, 68b, 69a, 69b, 70a, 70b; G. King, 118a; A. Lackner, 112a; D. & M. Lukehurst, 37; Lydd Cricket Club, 100a; J. Malyon, 119a; D. Mattock, 11b, 15b, 47b, 75, 76b, 77a, 101a, 102b; T. Miller, 121a; Ministry of Defence, 80b; S. Mirley, 96b; D. Moore, 100b; E. Niedrich, 36b; Nuclear Electric, 49, 51a, 51b, 52b; A. Paine, 45a, 45b, 102a; S. Paine, 50a, 57a, 110; H. Pierce, 40a, 41b, 105b; I. Pierce, 92b; J.C. Pilcher, 115, 116a, 116b, 118b; J.F. Pilcher, 83a, 92a; C. Pumphrey, 97a, 99b; M. Ralph, 123a; L. Ramsden, 39a, 39b, 40b; S. Ramsden, 19a, 19b, 20a, 21a, 35a; J. Roy, 25b; S. Sharp, 14a, 91a, 91b; N. Sims, 36a, 98b; J. Sinden, 26a, 30b, 31a, 31b, 32a, 32b, 38b, 41a, 42a, 88a, 117a; W. Smith, 82, 82b, 87; T. Standen, 76a, 78a; E.L. Tart, 4; P. Tidd, 122a; G. Warren, 48a, 62a, 86b, 93a, 93b; M. Williams, 68a, P. Winkfield, 59; and G. Woods, 20b, 22a, 22b, 33. All the remaining photographs are from the author's own collection.

# BRITAIN IN OLD PHOTOGRAPHS

Aberystwyth & North Ceredigion
Around Abingdon
Acton
Alderney: A Second Selection
Along the Avon from Stratford to Tewkesbury
Altrincham
Amersham
Around Amesbury
Anglesey
Arnold & Bestwood
Arnold & Bestwood: A Second Selection
Arundel & the Arun Valley
Ashbourne
Around Ashby-de-la-Zouch
Avro Aircraft
Aylesbury
Balham & Tooting
Banburyshire
Barnes, Mortlake & Sheen
Barnsley
Bath
Beaconsfield
Bedford
Bedfordshire at Work
Bedworth
Beverley
Bexley
Bideford
Bilston
Birmingham Railways
Bishop's Stortford & Sawbridgeworth
Bishopstone & Seaford
Bishopstone & Seaford: A Second Selection
Black Country Aviation
Black Country Railways
Black Country Road Transport
Blackburn
Blackpool
Around Blandford Forum
Bletchley
Bolton
Bournemouth
Bradford
Braintree & Bocking at Work
Brecon
Brentwood
Bridgwater & the River Parrett
Bridlington
Bridport & the Bride Valley
Brierley Hill
Brighton & Hove
Brighton & Hove: A Second Selection
Bristol
Around Bristol
Brixton & Norwood
Early Broadstairs & St Peters
Bromley, Keston & Hayes

Buckingham & District
Burford
Bury
Bushbury
Camberwell
Cambridge
Cannock Yesterday & Today
Canterbury: A Second Selection
Castle Combe to Malmesbury
Chadwell Heath
Chard & Ilminster
Chatham Dockyard
Chatham & Gillingham
Cheadle
Cheam & Belmont
Chelmsford
Cheltenham: A Second Selection
Cheltenham at War
Cheltenham in the 1950s
Chepstow & the River Wye
Chesham Yesterday & Today
Cheshire Railways
Chester
Chippenham & Lacock
Chiswick
Chorley & District
Cirencester
Around Cirencester
Clacton-on-Sea
Around Clitheroe
Clwyd Railways
Clydesdale
Colchester
Colchester 1940–70
Colyton & Seaton
The Cornish Coast
Corsham & Box
The North Cotswolds
Coventry: A Second Selection
Around Coventry
Cowes & East Cowes
Crawley New Town
Around Crawley
Crewkerne & the Ham Stone Villages
Cromer
Croydon
Crystal Palace, Penge & Anerley
Darlington
Darlington: A Second Selection
Dawlish & Teignmouth
Deal
Derby
Around Devizes
Devon Aerodromes
East Devon at War
Around Didcot & the Hagbournes
Dorchester
Douglas
Dumfries
Dundee at Work
Durham People

Durham at Work
Ealing & Northfields
East Grinstead
East Ham
Eastbourne
Elgin
Eltham
Ely
Enfield
Around Epsom
Esher
Evesham to Bredon
Exeter
Exmouth & Budleigh Salterton
Fairey Aircraft
Falmouth
Farnborough
Farnham: A Second Selection
Fleetwood
Folkestone: A Second Selection
Folkestone: A Third Selection
The Forest of Dean
Frome
Fulham
Galashiels
Garsington
Around Garstang
Around Gillingham
Gloucester
Gloucester: from the Walwin Collection
North Gloucestershire at War
South Gloucestershire at War
Gosport
Goudhurst to Tenterden
Grantham
Gravesend
Around Gravesham
Around Grays
Great Yarmouth
Great Yarmouth: A Second Selection
Greenwich & Woolwich
Grimsby
Around Grimsby
Grimsby Docks
Gwynedd Railways
Hackney: A Second Selection
Hackney: A Third Selection
From Haldon to Mid-Dartmoor
Hammersmith & Shepherds Bush
Hampstead to Primrose Hill
Harrow & Pinner
Hastings
Hastings: A Second Selection
Haverfordwest
Hayes & West Drayton
Around Haywards Heath
Around Heathfield
Around Heathfield: A Second Selection
Around Helston

Around Henley-on-Thames
Herefordshire
Herne Bay
Heywood
The High Weald
The High Weald: A Second Selection
Around Highworth
Around Highworth & Faringdon
Hitchin
Holderness
Honiton & the Otter Valley
Horsham & District
Houghton-le-Spring & Hetton-le-Hole
Houghton-le-Spring & Hetton-le-Hole: A Second Selection
Huddersfield: A Second Selection
Huddersfield: A Third Selection
Ilford
Ilfracombe
Ipswich: A Second Selection
Islington
Jersey: A Third Selection
Kendal
Kensington & Chelsea
East Kent at War
Keswick & the Central Lakes
Around Keynsham & Saltford
The Changing Face of Keynsham
Kingsbridge
Kingston
Kinver
Kirkby & District
Kirkby Lonsdale
Around Kirkham
Knowle & Dorridge
The Lake Counties at Work
Lancashire
The Lancashire Coast
Lancashire North of the Sands
Lancashire Railways
East Lancashire at War
Around Lancaster
Lancing & Sompting
Around Leamington Spa
Around Leamington Spa: A Second Selection
Leeds in the News
Leeds Road & Rail
Around Leek
Leicester
The Changing Face of Leicester
Leicester at Work
Leicestershire People
Around Leighton Buzzard & Linslade
Letchworth
Lewes
Lewisham & Deptford: A Second Selection
Lichfield

Lincoln
Lincoln Cathedral
The Lincolnshire Coast
Liverpool
Around Llandudno
Around Lochaber
Theatrical London
Around Louth
The Lower Fal Estuary
Lowestoft
Luton
Lympne Airfield
Lytham St Annes
Maidenhead
Around Maidenhead
Around Malvern
Manchester
Manchester Road & Rail
Mansfield
Marlborough: A Second Selection
Marylebone & Paddington
Around Matlock
Melton Mowbray
Around Melksham
The Mendips
Merton & Morden
Middlesbrough
Midsomer Norton & Radstock
Around Mildenhall
Milton Keynes
Minehead
Monmouth & the River Wye
The Nadder Valley
Newark
Around Newark
Newbury
Newport, Isle of Wight
The Norfolk Broads
Norfolk at War
North Fylde
North Lambeth
North Walsham & District
Northallerton
Northampton
Around Norwich
Nottingham 1944–74
The Changing Face of Nottingham
Victorian Nottingham
Nottingham Yesterday & Today
Nuneaton
Around Oakham
Ormskirk & District
Otley & District
Oxford: The University
Oxford Yesterday & Today
Oxfordshire Railways: A Second Selection
Oxfordshire at School
Around Padstow
Pattingham & Wombourne
Penwith
Penzance & Newlyn
Around Pershore
Around Plymouth
Poole
Portsmouth
Poulton-le-Fylde
Preston
Prestwich
Pudsey
Radcliffe
RAF Chivenor
RAF Cosford
RAF Hawkinge
RAF Manston
RAF Manston: A Second Selection
RAF St Mawgan
RAF Tangmere
Ramsgate & Thanet Life
Reading
Reading: A Second Selection
Redditch & the Needle District
Redditch: A Second Selection
Richmond, Surrey
Rickmansworth
Around Ripley
The River Soar
Romney Marsh
Romney Marsh: A Second Selection
Rossendale
Around Rotherham
Rugby
Around Rugeley
Ruislip
Around Ryde
St Albans
St Andrews
Salford
Salisbury
Salisbury: A Second Selection
Salisbury: A Third Selection
Around Salisbury
Sandhurst & Crowthorne
Sandown & Shanklin
Sandwich
Scarborough
Scunthorpe
Seaton, Lyme Regis & Axminster
Around Seaton & Sidmouth
Sedgley & District
The Severn Vale
Sherwood Forest
Shrewsbury
Shrewsbury: A Second Selection
Shropshire Railways
Skegness
Around Skegness
Skipton & the Dales
Around Slough
Smethwick
Somerton & Langport
Southampton
Southend-on-Sea
Southport
Southwark
Southwell
Southwold to Aldeburgh
Stafford
Around Stafford
Staffordshire Railways
Around Staveley
Stepney
Stevenage
The History of Stilton Cheese
Stoke-on-Trent
Stoke Newington
Stonehouse to Painswick
Around Stony Stratford
Around Stony Stratford: A Second Selection
Stowmarket
Streatham
Stroud & the Five Valleys
Stroud & the Five Valleys: A Second Selection
Stroud's Golden Valley
The Stroudwater and Thames & Severn Canals
The Stroudwater and Thames & Severn Canals: A Second Selection
Suffolk at Work
Suffolk at Work: A Second Selection
The Heart of Suffolk
Sunderland
Sutton
Swansea
Swindon: A Third Selection
Swindon: A Fifth Selection
Around Tamworth
Taunton
Around Taunton
Teesdale
Teesdale: A Second Selection
Tenbury Wells
Around Tettenhall & Codshall
Tewkesbury & the Vale of Gloucester
Thame to Watlington
Around Thatcham
Around Thirsk
Thornbury to Berkeley
Tipton
Around Tonbridge
Trowbridge
Around Truro
TT Races
Tunbridge Wells
Tunbridge Wells: A Second Selection
Twickenham
Uley, Dursley & Cam
The Upper Fal
The Upper Tywi Valley
Uxbridge, Hillingdon & Cowley
The Vale of Belvoir
The Vale of Conway
Ventnor
Wakefield
Wallingford
Walsall
Waltham Abbey
Wandsworth at War
Wantage, Faringdon & the Vale Villages
Around Warwick
Weardale
Weardale: A Second Selection
Wednesbury
Wells
Welshpool
West Bromwich
West Wight
Weston-super-Mare
Around Weston-super-Mare
Weymouth & Portland
Around Wheatley
Around Whetstone
Whitchurch to Market Drayton
Around Whitstable
Wigton & the Solway Plain
Willesden
Around Wilton
Wimbledon
Around Windsor
Wingham, Addisham & Littlebourne
Wisbech
Witham & District
Witney
Around Witney
The Witney District
Wokingham
Around Woodbridge
Around Woodstock
Woolwich
Woolwich Royal Arsenal
Around Wootton Bassett, Cricklade & Purton
Worcester
Worcester in a Day
Around Worcester
Worcestershire at Work
Around Worthing
Wotton-under-Edge to Chipping Sodbury
Wymondham & Attleborough
The Yorkshire Wolds